The Wi

Men..l ..i..s for

Maximum Performance

[Cherokee Trail Ed.]

by Jim Winges

Titan Sport Performance

Titan Sport Performance
www.facebook.com/Titan-Sport-Performance-1531757693598631
Colorado/New York

ISBN: 9798864979846

The Wrestling Edge

Technique

Cherokee
Trail
Wrestling

"Unless you continually work, evolve, and innovate, you'll Learn a quick and painful lesson from someone who has."
-Cael Sanderson

Foreword

'Building Champions On And Off The Mat'

I am very fortunate to have been introduced to Dr. Jim Winges five years ago at the Mile High Wrestling practice. Sonny and Cody Yohn (current Mile High Wrestling coaches, and NCAA All-American Wrestlers from the University of Minnesota) worked with Dr. Jim while wrestling in college. Dr. Jim has worked with Olympic, professional, college and high school athletes on developing the mental skills needed for each athlete to reach their full potential.

Dr. Winges recently worked with my son Matthew, who finished as the 5A 160 lb. State runner up in 2022. Matthew worked very closely and still works with Dr. Jim on controlling his mindset in his college wrestling. The mental edge in sports is key to having athletes excel in wrestling. Wrestling requires athletes to have superior physical attributes, but more importantly it requires the mental edge needed to compete at the highest level. Dr. Jim helped Matthew develop a positive mindset through practices and procedures that Matthew applied throughout his senior year to overcome the many obstacles he faced during his season. I have no doubt in my mind that the lessons he learned from Dr. Winges helped Matthew become one of the stop wrestlers in state his senior year.

I have been very fortunate and privileged to be able to compete and coach wrestling over the last 45 years. Wrestling has taught me many valuable lessons that have helped me overcome the many hurdles that life has thrown at me. Wrestling has taught me **Discipline, Desire, Dedication**, and the **Determination** needed to be successful on and off the wrestling mat. These D's are essential to becoming a champion on and off the mat. Dr. Winges has put together an incredible book that will help each wrestler achieve his goals and focus on the 4 D's of wrestling. This book will be easily accessible to our wrestlers, parents, and coaches. The book will provide a foundation for our wrestlers to develop a strong mindset that will help them overcome the obstacles they face during the wrestling season and in life.

I am super excited about this opportunity for our wrestlers. "The Wrestling Edge: Mental Skills for Maximum Performance" offers our coaches, wrestlers, and parents an opportunity to have a mental edge that is needed to be successful. Thank you Dr. Winges for your time and effort with the Cherokee Trail Wrestlers and Coaches.

Jeff Buck
Head Wrestling Coach, Cherokee Trail High School

Weight Management for Superior Wrestling
By Coach Jeff Buck

Cherokee Trail Wrestling:
"Building Champions on and off the Mat"

Cherokee Trail Wrestling promotes sound practices and belief that when wrestlers engage in weight loss, and it is done in a healthy way, the wrestler can become stronger and more competitive in a lower weight class. However, this is not mandatory or required practice in our program.

As a former student athlete, and current head coach, I believe that all coaches, parents, and athletes must be educated about the dangers of cutting weight including dehydration, use of laxatives, self-induced vomiting, starvation, sauna suits and steam rooms.

According to the 2022-2023 "NFHS Wrestling Rules outline the process for discouraging excessive weight loss and establishing a safe minimum weight which involves the wrestler, parent/guardians, appropriate health-care professional, and coach. An ideal program would be one where an appropriate health-care professional would assist in establishing a minimum weight class through hydration testing prior to the beginning of the season combined with body fat assessment and monitored decent plan. Minimum body fat should not be lower than seven percent for males". NFHS (Rule 1, Section 5, Articles 1-3).

The primary purpose of the weight certification program is to assist wrestlers in determining the weight class that is best for them, based on their current body composition. The certification process will also result in wrestlers receiving a weight loss descent plan. Per CHSAA regulations, all wrestlers losing weight must follow the descent plan. The decent plan will help them by providing clear guidance on what they should be weighing each week to descend safely to the lower weight classification.

The goal of Cherokee Trail Wrestling is to help our athletes compete at the highest levels. Cutting too much weight can have a negative impact on an athletes' performance. It is very important that all coaches, wrestlers, and parents work together in assisting every wrestler in wrestling the best weight class to help be successful by following safe weight management procedures such as safe hydration practices, good nutrition, strength training, and skill training. Cherokee Trail Wrestling will follow all guidelines set by CHSAA and the NFHS.

The Superior Wrestlers Diet

by Matthew Buck, former Cherokee Trail Wrestler, State Finalist, and current California Baptist University wrestler.

It is recommended that you follow this diet. Remember, you want to keep your metabolism moving so don't skip meals and **DRINK PLENTY OF WATER** (stay away from sugary drinks like soda and fruit juices). As you get closer to weigh-ins, you must begin to reduce the amount of water you drink. For example, I drink as much water as I can (divide your body weight in half and drink that many ounces, no excuses) from the time weigh-ins are completed until 24 hours prior to the next weigh-in. The more hydrated you are, the more weight you will lose. It is also recommended that you bring an extra t-shirt practice so you can change it during practice. You will lose more weight soaking two shirts versus putting on sweatpants/sweatshirt and overheating during practice. Coaches will tell you when you can put on long-sleeve shirts, and or sweats.

Morning Meal:
Many options including a meal replacement shake, bowl of oatmeal, 2-3 eggs. Stay away from foods high in carbs. Try to up your protein intake for this meal.

Mid Moring Snack:
A piece of fruit (apple, orange, 2-3 cuties, or banana)

Lunch:
Turkey, ham, or tuna Sandwich. Whole Wheat bread is the best, and you can add cheese, lettuce, tomato, BUT go light on the condiments. A wrestler can also make a nice salad with some sort of meat but go easy on the dressing.

Mid Afternoon Snack:
Piece or fruit, vegetables, and/or protein shake, or protein bar.

After Practice:
Water or Gatorade.

9

Dinner:
Piece of lean meat, salad, and vegetables. You can eat pasta but
limit that to 1 cup. Remember, the more water you drink the better.
You do not want to get dehydrated. I also recommend you bring
sweatshirt or sweatpants, so once practice is finished you can spend
EXTRA time doing a bike workout or put on your running shoes and
run two miles. I would do at least 15 minutes each day of
extras work (extra running does not include the running that the team
does). Lifting weights THREE times a week is also important.
Lifting can include pullups, pushups, air squats etc. **The more you
run, the more you can eat and the better shape you will be in.**

Always try and stay within FOUR pounds of your wrestling weight if
you 120lbs and below. FIVE to SIX pounds if you are between 125-
175lbs. And SEVEN to EIGHT pounds if you are an upper weight.
I am referring to your weight when you check Monday morning. Be
sure to check your weight every day at practice.

The Wrestling Edge

Introduction

The Wrestling Edge was developed to assist wrestlers in their training, style, philosophy, and performance. It is a straight-to-the-point set of proven techniques to improve wrestling performance.

Across a wrestler's career, a very small percentage of training time is spent working on the mental side of their game. In fact, most wrestlers actively spend less than 5% of their training time working on their mental skills.

It is important to understand that as we move up in level, the physical, tactical, and technical differences between wrestlers tends to wash out because everyone is tactically proficient, technically good, physically in-shape, and at the highest levels they are also often physically gifted. This is unfortunate because the reality of sport is that there is typically less than a 5% difference in size, strength, and speed among wrestlers of a given level and weight class. What separates the champions from the other physically talented wrestlers is the mental side of wrestling. The bottom line is that wrestlers who work on the mental side of their game do better in practice and competition, get more mat time, report fewer injuries and receive more accolades than wrestlers who do not put effort into developing their mental skills. Mentally strong wrestlers are better able to handle the stress and adversity of wrestling and thus perform better and have more fun and less stress while doing it.

What are mental skills? Mental skills are the tools and techniques you will learn or develop that go beyond physical, technical, and tactical training to make you a better, more complete wrestler. Think of your skillset as a toolbox. Every physical, technical, tactical, and mental technique you have learned over your many years training and competing is a tool in that toolbox. The wrestler with more tools is better able to handle the adversity they will inevitably experience in their wrestling career. Some of our mental skills and techniques include:

- Stress Management
- Arousal Management
- Self-Confidence
- Managing Negative Thoughts
- Emotional Control
- Relaxation Abilities
- Imagery Abilities
- Mental Toughness
- Resilience
- Philosophies for High Performance
- Mindset
- Positivity
- Focus
- Creation and Development of Routines
- Goal Setting
- Recovery protocols
- And many more

These are the mental skills that allow a wrestler to reach their full athletic potential and maximize their performance, status, accolades, and potential earnings across their career.

The process of learning mental skills and techniques is simple enough. Open your mind to the techniques, practice them and utilize those that work for you. Even if you do not need a particular skill right now, you can develop it and store it away in your toolbox for later. Unexpected situations arise, often at big competitions and our toolbox of mental skills can provide us with the tools to deal with the situation and still perform at a high level and achieve success and hopefully a championship. You may want to approach this program like a pirate; take what you want from this program and use it to become a better wrestler...store the rest in your treasure chest for later. Most wrestlers can improve their performance 10-30% in a short span of time simply by engaging in mental skills training wholeheartedly. My suggestion is that you go through the book in order the first time to familiarize yourself with all of the techniques and complete the assignments. Then go back to specific techniques as you need them.

Strengths and Weaknesses

It is often beneficial to begin one's journey in mental skills training with a critical analysis of our strengths and weaknesses as a wrestler. Understanding your strengths and weaknesses will often sharpen your focus when learning the subsequent techniques highlighted in this book.

Assignment:
Think about your strengths and weaknesses as a wrestler and list them below. These items can be physical, mental, technical, or tactical.

Strengths

-

-

-

Weaknesses

-

-

-

Your Strengths should give you confidence and represent something you can draw upon when facing adversity. For instance, I have a great armbar setup or I have great footwork on my takedowns. Weaknesses should be something you work on daily in practice to improve your performance.

Along with our strengths and weaknesses it is also important to know about our mental skills. Rate yourself on the following mental skills on a scale from 1 to 10. Ten being the very best you can be.

Self Confidence _____

Effort _____

Attention to Detail _____

Focus _____

GRIT _____

Communication _____

Great Attitude _____

Ability to Relax _____

Ability to Visualize _____

Preparation _____

Managing Worry _____

Motivation _____

Stress Management _____

Resilience _____

Energy_____

Now look over your scores. Ideally, we want all of these scores to be in the 9-10 range. Any time we score lower than a 5 it represents a problem area that we need to work on. Revisit this list after you have completed this book and practiced the techniques. You'll likely find that your scores have improved.

Another important assessment is your move-set and its diversity. Typically, a high school wrestler can get by and even win State with two really good take downs. In college he/she might need 3-4 that they are highly proficient at to be competitive and go to NCAA's. At the world level they may need 5-8 to be competitive and challenge for a championship. I always encourage wrestlers to be ahead of their level. Take the time to develop 1 level up for take downs, take down defense, top position moves, escape moves, and reversal moves. This is often best completed in the off season or pre-season. Adding to your move-set will make you a bigger threat and give you more options in securing the win.

Player Persona

Many wrestlers benefit from creating a persona on which to base their athletic identity. Wrestlers can model their persona after superheroes, mythical warriors, or world champions. You can think of the persona as the core to which you attach all of your physical, technical, tactical, and mental skills. We try to take on the attributes of that persona and embody it. Often when we are underperforming, feel panicked, out of control, or under-motivated, we can go back to our persona and adjust our responses to match how our chosen persona would respond. For example, one could ask themselves how Cael Sanderson, Jordan Burroughs, Dan Gable, Saori Yoshida, Kyle Dake handle a situation. Some personas that athletes have successfully used in the past include:

The Superhero
o Wonder Woman - pure of heart, powerful, unstoppable, agile, leads by example.
o Batman – intellectual, versatile, physically adept, agility
o Superman– agility, super strength, team player.
o Goku – ultimate competitor, adaptor, immense effort, never satisfied.

The Samurai – honor, commitment, development of mind and body, learning, adaptability (i.e., Miyamoto Musashi). For females, Onna-bugeisha were female samurai who fought side by side with their male counterparts with a similar mentality.

The Warrior for God/Family – blood, sweat, and tears shed to honor god and/or family, to lift one's god or family up. Someone of great courage and self-discipline.

A Role Model – Usually a world champion wrestler or coach, who embodies everything that is good about wrestling. The only issue is that sometimes our role models let us down...so choose your role model very carefully. The main point here is that we can learn to take on some of the qualities and attributes of our chosen persona to assist us in being a better athlete and improving our performance.

My Persona: _____

Attributes that will enhance my development and performance:

-
-

-
-

-
-

-
-

-
-

Assignment

As you move forward in your wrestling, try to embody your persona. If you find you are having an off day at practice or in the heat of the moment you find yourself unsure of what do when facing adversity, ask yourself "*What would my persona do?*". If you have chosen a good persona and embodied it in your wrestling, it will likely help you make the right decision that will lead to a victory rather than defeat.

As we move forward in this book, remember to blend each technique with your persona. If your persona embodies power and strength, then your techniques should embody those attributes as well.

Maximizing Performance Imagery

Imagery is visualization…or the use of your mind to imagine successful wrestling performances. Research has found that using imagery just prior to performing a sports skill increases the likelihood that that the performance of that skill will be successful. For instance, a wrestler using imagery might imagine themselves making a great takedown. And subsequently this makes it more likely for that takedown to be more successful when they actually perform it in a practice or a match. For some sports skills, the use of imagery can more than double the chances of having a successful performance. Imagery can be utilized both on and off the mat.

There are several tips of ways we can improve our imagery:

1. **Stay relaxed.** First, take some deep breaths. We typically image better when we are relaxed, and these deep breaths helps us relax…. especially if you've just been exerting yourself.

2. **Images must always be positive.** If you engage in imagery and it comes out negatively…repeat it again making sure you get a positive result during the imagery. In your mind you should always be the most <u>dominant</u> wrestler and <u>unstoppable</u>. If you perform after a negative image there is a very high chance that you will have a negative performance, so keep it <u>positive</u>!

3. **Image from multiple perspectives.** Learn how to image from both first-person (as if looking out of your own eyes) and third-person (as if we're watching ourselves on TV) perspectives. If you can't do both right now, just focus on getting your preferred perspective stronger before moving to develop the other.

4. **Create 'rich' images.** Rich images utilize all of our senses and attempt to make the imagery as real as possible.

19

- o Hearing – Image the sounds of the match. *Hear* the heavy breathing, the thump of bodies clashing, the sound of the crowd at the tournament.

- o Sight - Image *seeing* your opponent, the mat, the arena, the path or flow of moves to create your victory.

- o Touch – Image the *feel* of your gear, the mat, and your opponent's mass and strength. Feel the moves you want to make.

- o Smell – Image the s*mell* of the arena and the tension in the air.

- o Taste – Image the *taste* of the Gatorade/Powerade/Water on your tongue. *Taste* the sweat on your lip.

By creating rich images, we are transporting ourselves into the match where we are <u>dominant</u> and <u>always compete well</u>. This subsequently raises our confidence and performance. If you win 20-30 matches in your head a day it is going to improve your confidence.

5. **Use imagery during the short breaks in the match or when you are awaiting your match.** Take a split second to image as you wait to wrestle again after a restart.

6. **Use imagery at home.** A great way to develop self-confidence is to image after a progressive muscle relaxation session (described in the next chapter). Image yourself performing perfectly and dominating the match. Doing so not only improves our imagery ability but also strengthens the mental aspects of our tactical and technical skills via mental rehearsal. Imagery enhances what is often referred to as muscle memory.

<u>Extreme Imagery</u>

An alternative form of imagery is *extreme imagery*. Extreme imagery is a self-confidence builder where one imagines themselves with superhuman strength, explosiveness, and speed. For extreme imagery you could imagine that you are so explosive that you can get a single or double leg before your opponent even has a chance to react. One could think of this as a form of mental overspeed training. You could also imagine yourself with the power and strength to easily break your opponent's defense. Imaging such things can be fun and can raise our confidence. A very simple example of this when used for MMA is imagining punching an opponent so hard, the he/she flies through the cage, crowd and out the side of the arena. This is often seen in anime or superhero shows. Extreme imagery can be useful, but you should still follow all of the tips listed on the previous page for standard imagery, just to an almost ridiculous level of intensity. Extreme imagery is not the foundation of your imagery skills. It is a complement to an already great imagery skillset.

So how do you incorporate imagery?
- o One the mat a wrestler can take a split second to image just prior to performing a takedown setup, or submission setup.
- o Off the mat, wrestlers will typically lay in a comfortable position and take 5-10 minutes imagining themselves making great moves that follow their own style of wrestling. Some high-level competitors take this very seriously… completing an upcoming match in their mind several times before actually beginning the match.

ALWAYS REMEMBER THAT IN YOUR MIND YOU ARE THE BEST WRESTLER EVER…YOU ARE DOMINANT, AND YOU COMPETE WITHOUT ERROR.

Assignment

Spend 10-30 minutes a day engaging in rich, positive imagery. Imagine yourself making great takedowns, moves, and defenses.

Progressive Muscle Relaxation

Progressive muscle relaxation (PMR) is a relaxation technique used by wrestlers to relax their bodies. With practice, PMR training allows athletes to gain a specialized skill to completely relax their body on command. This is especially advantageous for high pressure performance situations like wrestling matches.

Ideally PMR is done in a quiet place where the wrestler can be as comfortable as possible. To begin, sit or lie down in a comfortable position. In general, one begins with deep breathing exercises. After a short period (1-2 minutes) of deep breathing, the athlete contracts a particular muscle, holding that contraction for about 10-12 seconds. After this time the athlete <u>releases the contraction</u> thinking about the word *relax* and the sensation of any pain, inflammation, anger, frustration, and/or stress <u>leaving their body</u>. In a 12-minute PMR session the wrestler will typically go through the contraction-relaxation cycle twice for each of the following muscle groups, in series: calves, quads, abdominals, chest/arms/fists together, and the traps.

After completion of a PMR session, the whole body is relaxed. More importantly, you are learning how it feels to be that relaxed and what it takes to get there. By practicing PMR you will gain the ability to relax your body <u>on command</u>. It is suggested that wrestlers use a PMR MP3 to guide them through the process, so they do not have to think about what to do next during the contraction phase, resulting in maximal relaxation for the beginner. To learn the skill of relaxation, wrestlers should engage in PMR six nights a week right before bed for the first 3-4 weeks. After this initial period, they can taper back to 3-4 nights a week. Relaxation is a skill that must be maintained so I suggest wrestlers engage in a minimum of 3-4 sessions of PMR a week for the remainder of their competition careers.

PMR will not only relax you right before bed but also to get you better sleep. Many wrestlers will fall asleep while doing PMR. That's okay because getting more sleep is beneficial for performance as well. However, if you don't fall asleep, you will start to gain the ability to relax on command. You can use this technique to relax your body in practice and matches with one deep breath and contraction of a single muscle of your choosing. This is a highly valued skill in sport since it allows us to manipulate our arousal, reduce stress, and maintain focus. Some athletes are so good at this skill that they can manipulate their heart rate during competition for faster recovery. For instance, a highly trained athlete can drop their heart rate from approximately 180 bpm to 70 bpm in about six seconds. Utilizing this skill would allow the athlete to be more ready for the upcoming action after a restart or break. This gives you an advantage over your opponent who hasn't likely trained mentally to do this.

Note: Wrestlers who don't fall asleep will find themselves in a state that allows them to fall asleep faster. PMR is an excellent tool when traveling for competitions and staying in hotel rooms where it can be difficult to sleep. It effectively primes us for sleep.

Assignment

Add the two .mp3 files from Dr. Winges' share drive to your phone and then engage in PMR six nights a week right before bed for the next 3-4 weeks. After that you can taper it down to 3-4 times a week. After the first 3-4 weeks, begin using deep breathing in practice and a quick 10 second flex to relax in practice. Once you are used to using it in practice, begin using it in matches.

Progressive Muscle Relaxation MP3
https://share.getcloudapp.com/YEu87eBL#

Healing Imagery MP3
https://share.getcloudapp.com/6qu0jbZm#

Healing Imagery is a very high-level skill where we can learn to control the blood flow in the body and enhance healing and recovery. If you are injured, try the Healing Imagery MP3 above and listen and attempt to get in touch with your injury and send healing energy and nutrients to your injury during each inhale and removing pain and inflammation from the injury with each exhale. Imagine your injured muscles or bones stitching themselves back together stronger than they ever were before. Athletes who learn this technique can shave months off their recovery time for severe injuries.

Recover Faster!
Maximizing Natural HGH Production

Human Growth Hormone (HGH) is widely considered the fountain of youth for athletes in nearly all sports. HGH not only allows us to build muscle, it also allows us to recover from the previous day's workout at an enhanced rate. The combination of increased muscle recovery and increased mass building means that athletes can continue to grow and improve at a very high rate. This is highly valuable to combat sport athletes in sports like wrestling, judo, jiu-jitsu and MMA.

How do we get HGH?

1. Artificially – This is illegal in all major sports and against WADA and Government regulations. It is also highly dangerous and linked to cancer in this form.

2. Naturally - Our bodies naturally produce it in response to exercise and during sleep!

Since we naturally produce HGH it is beneficial for athletes to learn how they can maximize natural HGH production in their own bodies.

HGH production in the body is tied to sleep. In particular, deep sleep. Its production begins during stage 3 sleep and peaks 3-4 hours into your uninterrupted sleep (see figure on following page). At this point HGH production ramps up quickly but only continues at a high rate while the athlete has UNINTERRUPTED sleep. Any interruption in sleep results in a near halt to HGH production until stage 3 (deep) sleep is regained. Sleep interruptions such as bathroom needs, roommate/significant other disturbances, pet disturbances and sleep environment disturbances dramatically reduce overall HGH production.

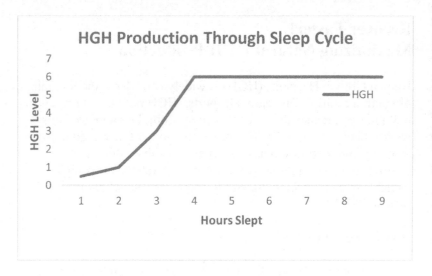

HGH Production Through Sleep Cycle

Therefore, it is essential that wrestlers engage in large amounts of uninterrupted sleep to maximize HGH production which will then maximize recovery from that day's workout and improve mass building, metabolism and body repair capabilities. Ideally, athletes should have 8-10 hours of sleep per day. Some studies show 10% or more improvement in performance for wrestlers who are getting 10 hours of sleep. Wrestlers maximizing HGH production are able to continually increase the difficulty of their workouts while still being able to recover from them. Higher difficulty workouts combined with enhanced mass building result in much greater gains verse wrestlers not getting enough sleep and lower HGH.

Sleep is the new secret weapon of pro sports teams. Some pro teams are putting large amounts of resources into helping their athletes get more sleep, even going so far as tracking players sleep via wearable technology. By tracking player sleep data, strength coaches can push athletes more and coaches can make better decisions regarding playing time. Getting more sleep is also why most college sports teams put their athletes in hotels for home games and give players a curfew. Coaches know that getting enough sleep is very important to athlete performance. These same principles can be utilized to enhance your development as a wrestler.

Assignment

Clear your sleep of disturbances and aim to achieve 8-10 hours of uninterrupted sleep each night. If you have wearable fitness technology utilize it to enhance your workouts. On days where you earned a high sleep score push yourself hard. In the space below, list the things that disrupt your sleep. How might you be able to fix these things?

Arousal Management – Never Play Flat Again!

One of the most important elements of high performance wrestling is the ability to manage and manipulate your arousal levels. You can be too amped up or too flat, which affects your performance. Not monitoring and controlling your arousal level means that you are leaving this highly important aspect of sport to chance. Wrestlers can have matches where they are nearly asleep and others when they are too amped up. This dramatically reduces the amount of time that they are *in the zone* or what sport psychologists call *flow*. Being in the zone/flow is a state where we are so focused and into our match, that everything just happens almost on autopilot. We typically have our best performance when we're in the zone and flow. When this happens, we feel faster, stronger, and anticipate opponent tactics almost before they happen. You've all seen a Wrestler who takes over a match stumping their opponent. She/he was likely in flow. If you are in flow, it is highly likely that you will win the match.

Unfortunately, even the best wrestlers are only in the zone/flow for about 30% of the time during their career. The best wrestlers realize this and learn to control arousal, so they are as close to the zone/flow as possible. In doing so, it might only take a single thing or two to go right and they move them into the zone/flow where they can then take over the match and dominate.

The graphics below illustrate the inverted U relationship between psychological arousal (mental energy) and performance. As we become more psychologically aroused, performance improves but only to a certain point. After that point performance begins to decline. And for some people that decline can look like falling off a cliffs edge.

What's important here is knowing where your personal arousal levels need to be, and how to get there so you are *in the zone* or as close as possible as much as possible.

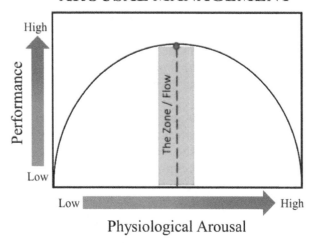

Everyone has a perfect range of arousal and optimal performance they can achieve at the perfect arousal level. A large part of your job as a wrestler is to find it!

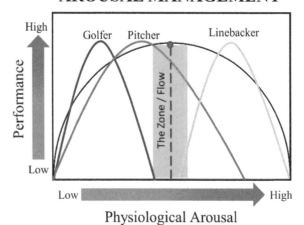

The previous figure illustrates that <u>different people</u> and <u>different positions</u> in a sport have different curves and psychological arousal needs. Note that everyone has their own perfect arousal level where performance is highest. In general, a golfer would likely need lower arousal (higher calmness) than the goalie or linebacker. What is important here is that you find <u>your perfect spot</u> and learn how to get there and stay there before and during matches.

Getting and Staying in the Zone

Learning how to get to the perfect arousal point and range (the green highlighted area) allows wrestlers to perform better, have more fun, and they tend to be more successful in reaching their goals. Getting there and staying there requires a <u>personal check-in</u>. A personal check-in is simply checking in with yourself and asking, "where am I on the curve?" which will put you in one of three categories:

1. <u>Too flat</u>: If you are flat (the left side of your personal curve), possibly sleepy and slow. You need to *amp up/ pump up* to increase your arousal.

2. <u>Too pumped up</u>: If you are too far on the right side of your personal curve you are likely too pumped up and might be feeling anxiety, nervousness, and lack of control. In this case you'll need to relax and calm down to bring yourself closer to that all-important green area of the zone.

3. <u>In the Zone</u>: You are in the green zone; aka flow and you should just roll with it. You are likely performing near your personal best.

Many wrestlers can dramatically improve their consistency and overall performance by engaging in this arousal management process. They also tend to have more fun and be less stressed and frustrated.

The graphic below illustrates some simple techniques to manipulate your arousal level.

AROUSAL MANAGEMENT

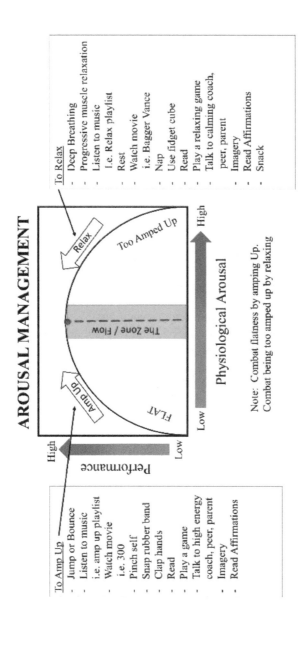

To Relax
- Deep Breathing
- Progressive muscle relaxation
- Listen to music
  i.e. Relax playlist
- Rest
- Watch movie
  i.e. Bagger Vance
- Nap
- Use fidget cube
- Read
- Play a relaxing game
- Talk to calming coach, peer, parent
- Imagery
- Read Affirmations
- Snack

To Amp Up
- Jump or Bounce
- Listen to music
  i.e. amp up playlist
- Watch movie
  i.e. 300
- Pinch self
- Snap rubber band
- Clap hands
- Read
- Play a game
- Talk to high energy coach, peer, parent
- Imagery
- Read Affirmations

Performance

High

Low

Relax

Too Amped Up

Amp Up

FLAT

The Zone / Flow

Physiological Arousal

High

Low

Note: Combat flatness by amping Up.
Combat being too amped up by relaxing

32

Assignments:

1. Create a 20 to 40-minute playlist of music that helps you **pump up**. Create a 20 to 40-minute playlist of music that helps you **calm down**. Add these playlists to your phone so you can take it with you when you travel. The further your travel the longer your playlists should be.

2. Add the Progressive Muscle Relaxation MP3 to your phone if you haven't already https://share.getcloudapp.com/YEu87eBL#

3. Think back to your personal best match. How was your arousal level…use this as a baseline until you can locate your perfect point and range.

4. Start performing personal check-ins 1-2 hours before all practices and matches and every 30 minutes after that. If you aren't *in the zone,* use a technique to get you closer.

5. During the match or tournament when there is a break in the action perform a quick check-in and respond accordingly using one of the techniques above.

6. During a match you can take a few seconds during the break to reduce your heart rate and ready yourself for the upcoming action.

7. What other ways can you pump yourself up or calm yourself down?

Pump Up

-
-
-
-
-
-
-

Calm Down

-
-
-
-
-
-
-

Arousal management inverted U is based on the work of Landers & Arent (2010).

Control the Controllables

Many wrestlers have difficulty managing the adversity that comes with wrestling. Control the Controllables (CTC) is a philosophy of sport and a way of life that can dramatically improve performance.

Take a moment and in the space below write down all of the things in wrestling that you do not have direct control over.

I cannot directly control (list in the space provided):

As you can see, we have a lot of things that we don't have direct control over in wrestling. Some of these include: the score, opponents, coaches, referees, parents, siblings, significant others, fans, teammates, the mat, hype, rankings, media, etc. We only have a certain amount of mental energy, and if we focus our mental energy on things outside our direct control it causes us to spin our wheels, stress out, and then perform poorly. Some wrestlers are so consumed by the *uncontrollables* that they experience anxiety and perform poorly. For instance, a wrestler who over focuses on rankings.

There is a better way. Please take a moment to think about the things that you <u>do have direct control</u> over. It is likely a much smaller list.

We have direct control over:
1. <u>Attitude</u> – your attitude is a choice...choose to have a positive attitude and perform better.

2. <u>Communication</u> – both listening and speaking...lack of communication in practice and matches stalls our development and loses matches. A important part of communication is not going on the defensive when receiving feedback.

3. <u>Effort</u> – effort is everything (100% effort, 100% of the time) ...you choose how much effort you put into training, practice, film work, and matches. If you want to be a champion, put in the effort to be one.

Note: I call the first three our A.C.E.

4. <u>Preparation</u> – there is no excuse for lack of preparation (film, gear, gym bag, food, your weight cut, stretching, recovery, etc.). Do an equipment check before you leave for practice and matches. Prepare like a champion.

5. <u>Nutrition</u> – you control how and what you put into your body…we are what we eat and how we fuel our bodies has a great effect on our overall performance.

You have direct control over the above five *controllables* in every aspect of your life. The CTC Philosophy compels us to focus our energy only on what we have direct control over. This allows us to manage stress, be happier, and perform at a higher level.

To achieve this, you must learn to be self-aware of your thoughts, feelings, and actions. Any thoughts, feelings and actions focused on things outside of our control should be stopped and eliminated. **Remind yourself to *control the controllables*.**
A few things to keep in mind:

1. While this is a simple philosophy, it is difficult to do. You will have challenges and often fail (maybe daily). That's okay! It's not whether you failed that's important… it's <u>how fast</u> you realize it and get back to only trying to control the controllables. Most people will fail daily…the best wrestlers realize it and get back to controlling the controllables as fast as possible.

2. Self-awareness is the key. You must catch yourself when you are focusing on things outside your control. Once you do – remind yourself to control the controllables and resume your life focusing on what you can control. Make the adjustment to better your situation.

You'll find that sport and life are much <u>easier</u> and <u>less stressful</u> when you control the controllables. In all honesty, *Controlling the Controllables* is probably the best piece of advice I can give to any wrestler for improving performance.

Assignment

Take control of your life and endeavor to control the controllables. Throughout your day ask yourself, "Am I controlling the controllables?" If not, focus on doing so. In the space below, list some of the situations in life that you traditionally don't control the controllables. In the future, be especially aware in these situations and remind yourself to control the controllables.

Controlling the controllables is based on the writings of Bull, Albinson, and Shambrook (2006).

Three Psychological Needs – What You Must Fulfill

As human beings we all have three psychological needs which must be fulfilled for us to be mentally well and perform at a high level. These needs are:

1. Competence – All wrestlers need to feel competent in what they do to perform well. Anytime we don't feel competent we perform poorly. Think about the last time your coach really chewed you out…she/he likely made you feel poorly and that increased your stress, making it difficult to perform your best. Yes, sometimes we need a kick in the pants to motivate us but when someone feels incompetent for long periods of time, they start to feel like they can do nothing right, they stress out, and perform poorly. Sometimes they will even burn out and drop out of wrestling all together.

2. Autonomy – All wrestlers need to feel like they have choices. A choice to practice, compete and recover. When a wrestler feels like they do not have choices it stresses them out, they perform poorly, and it becomes difficult to overcome the adversity that wrestling places in front of us.

3. Relatedness – All wrestlers need to feel that they are part of the group. If we don't feel like we are part of the group, we don't perform well - often because we aren't motivated, and we aren't as committed. If you are shy or new and not yet part of the group, try to reach out to teammates, coaches & staff. Try to find people with whom you enjoy spending time. Make it a goal to learn about your teammates and reach out to hang out with them.

When these three needs are met, wrestlers perform well and are typically happy. However, when one or more of the needs are not met, wrestlers often sink into poor performance and sometimes mental illness, maladaptation, and a host of other problems including: burnout, overtraining, depression, anxiety, suicidal thoughts, eating disorders, drug and alcohol abuse, and amoral or illegal behavior. Basically, nothing good is going to occur when the three needs are not met.

Groups supporting high level athletes including the United States Olympic Committee are investing heavily in working with athletes to help them fulfill the three psychological needs. They have had a great deal of success in helping their athletes perform better at the Olympic level. wrestling teams & camps would be wise to do the same for their wrestlers.

Assignment

Check in with yourself at least once a week and ask yourself if your three needs are being fulfilled. If they aren't, seek out help from your support people: Dr. Winges, your teams coach, staff, your family, or whoever you look to for support. **Make Certain You Fulfill Your Psychological Needs.** Life, and even more so our wrestling careers, are too short for us not to enjoy the ride!

Mindset – Choosing the Right Path

In recent years, the world's greatest teams in nearly all sports have placed a greater emphasis on 'Mindset.' Mindset can be summarized as a form of motivation and while it truly is a continuum of thoughts, goals, and behaviors. Sport psychologists typically describe mindset as two polar opposites to simplify it. It is up to the individual athlete to choose which of the two mindsets they wish to follow and bring to training and matches.

Fixed Mindset
As shown in the following graphic, the fixed mindset is typically associated with undesirable characteristics and attributes in wrestlers. To dramatically simplify it, a fixed mindset can be thought of as very closed-minded thinking. Fixed mindset individuals typically feel that performance is static and that they don't improve through practice…they rely on talent. They desire to look good and look smart. Any challenge to looking good and being smart causes them to typically shut down or lash out at others. Wrestlers with a fixed mindset don't want to be challenged and often give up and sometimes pretend to be injured when facing adversity. These individuals don't give much effort and rarely listen to feedback because they dislike it. They are also threatened by the success of others. Unfortunately, wrestlers with a fixed mindset never reach their full potential. The self-admitted quintessential fixed mindset athlete is John McEnroe. Even though he was the #1 ranked tennis player in the world for four years, in his mind he could do no wrong and failed to improve his game after achieving #1 status. He admits now that if he had been a growth mindset athlete, he would have been an even better tennis player and number one for far more years. Wrestlers would be wise to avoid this mindset.

Growth Mindset
At the other end of the continuum is growth mindset, which is associated with desirable wrestler characteristics. Growth mindset wrestlers truly believe that high performance is developed through practice. They are often thought of as human sponges because of their desire to learn. They soak up everything a coach says and learn

from it. Growth mindset wrestlers embrace challenge...it is why they are in the sport in the first place...to challenge themselves, thrive off adversity, and overcome obstacles. Effort is very important to the growth mindset wrestler, and they will rarely, if ever, take a play off or a day off. These wrestlers enjoy feedback and criticism because it offers them more information to improve. Growth mindset wrestlers are inspired by the success of others and when inspired it pushes them to work even harder. As a result of this mindset, these athletes reach ever-higher levels of achievement and performance. wrestlers would be wise to adopt and integrate these growth mindset characteristics into their personal style.

How can you change your mindset?
Like many techniques in sport psychology, self-awareness is key. Anytime you think or behave in a fixed mindset way, be aware of it and remind yourself to be more *growth* minded and alter your behavior to be consistent with the growth mindset. Do this enough and it will become a habit, and that habit will lead to better, stronger performances.

For example. If a wrestler has a very bad practice, they can look at it two primary ways.

1. Fixed Mindset – "I failed, and I am embarrassed, and I don't want to practice tomorrow." Or "I can't do anything right today so I'm just going to try and not get hurt." These are very negative and offer little room to improve.

OR

2. Growth Mindset – "It sucks that I failed today but that failure is going to push me tomorrow. I refuse to be beaten and will push harder to get better than I was today." This mindset offers an opportunity to grow, improve, and the motivational boost to push the wrestler to get there.

Fixed Mindset

Growth Mindset

Fixed Mindset		Growth Mindset
Performance is Static	**Believes**	Performance is Developed
To Look Good/Smart	**Desires**	To Learn & Improve
Avoids Challenges	**Challenges**	Embraces Challenges
Gets Defensive & Gives up	**Obstacles**	Persists & Overcomes Adversity
Effort is Fruitless	**Effort**	Effort is the Path to Mastery
Ignores Negative & Constructive Feedback	**Criticism**	Learns from Feedback
Threatened by Success of Others	**Success of Others**	Inspired by the Success of Others
Plateaus & Never Reaches Full Potential	**Result**	Ever-Higher Levels of Achievement & Performance

If you keep pushing with a Growth Mindset you will reach your goal.

Assignment:
Consider the following questions to form a plan to work towards having a growth mindset.

1. What opportunities are there for learning and growth today?

    -
    -
    -

2. When, where, and how will I act on my opportunity?

    -
    -
    -

3. What do I have to do to maintain and continue the growth?

    -
    -
    -

4. What skill will I focus on improving today?

    -
    -
    -

Mindset – choosing the right path, is based on the work by Dweck (2008).

Positive Body Language

Body Language is an essential component to mental toughness and high performance. Your body language not only affects your own self-confidence but also the confidence of your coach, teammates, and opponents. Body language also affects your wrestling, if a ref gives you a point, and if your opponent fears your skill and how they respond to the moves you make.

Positive, dominant body language for wrestling is about making yourself *BIG and powerful.* Your head should be up, shoulders back, arms out, feet shoulder width apart. When on the mat show a strong wrestling stance in the standup. Never let your opponent see you in pain, out of breath, frustrated, or hurt. It only fuels their confidence. Depending on the image you want to put forward, you can smile, or you can have your *game face* on in an attempt to intimidate. If you are in pain smile to hide it. Below is an example of an athlete with poor body language verse good body language before a practice.

Poor Body Language   *Big/Good Body Language*

Exhibiting negative body language is never going to help your wrestling performance.

Conversely, I've worked with many athletes who have increased their performance and playing time simply by changing their body language to be more positive. Positive body language enhances the confidence of yourself, your teammates, your coach and saps it away from your opponent. I like to think of it as fuel. I can either fuel my confidence by exhibiting great body language, which also intimidates and takes confidence away from our opponent, or I can fuel my opponent's confidence by showing poor body language and giving them confidence and the will to beat me. Which should we choose?

Eye contact is crucial. When you are receiving feedback, no matter how negative, <u>do not</u> break eye contact with your coach. Eye contact is an indicator that you are listening. Nodding to confirm that you understand helps as well. Little bothers a coach more than a wrestler that doesn't seem like they are listening or caring about their performance or enhancing their training partners performance.

Never, ever, argue with your coach on the mat. Take accountability for missteps even if you weren't completely at fault...doing so robs your opponent of the confidence they gain from seeing you argue. You can sort out the misstep later off the mat. Watch the greatest captains and leaders in any sport and they will often give the "that's on me" pat to their chest even when the mistake wasn't their own. These leaders are willing to sacrifice their ego for the betterment of the team and in doing so they maintain everyone's good body language, cohesion, and confidence.

Assignment
Analyze your own body language and write down some situations where you traditionally show poor body language. Make an effort to improve your body language. Maintain eye contact when receiving feedback from coaches. Pay close attention to your body language when things aren't going well.

Stopping Negative Thoughts

Many wrestlers have problems with negative thinking and negative images. Like the old Tom and Jerry cartoons we all have a little angel on one shoulder and a little devil on the other shoulder. The angel represents positive self-talk and helps build your self-confidence by reminding you that you are a great wrestler, competitor, and that you do things right. On the other shoulder is the little devil version of yourself. The devil chirps in our ear with negative comments like "you suck" "you can't" "you won't" "don't miss". We want to listen to the angel that builds us up and stop the comments from the devil that tears us down. To stop the devil, we engage in *negative thought stopping* or *Channel Changing.*

Two great methods to use for stopping negative thoughts are *negative thought stopping* and *channel changing.*

<u>Negative Thought Stopping</u> - is the active process of ending negative thoughts. For this method you first imagine a stop sign flashing in your mind anytime you have negative thoughts. This tells us to *stop* the negative thoughts. Next you can either a) change the negative thought to a positive one. For example, "You Suck!" becomes a positive like statement like "As long as I keep working hard, I will get better." Or b) *Stop* the negative thought and then image/visualize yourself taking turning & pinning an opponent or making a great takedown. I prefer option (b) because it is faster and more usable during competition.

<u>Channel Changing</u>. The idea is to think of your mind as a TV. If you don't like what's on your TV…then CHANGE THE CHANNEL to an image of you performing well. Think of it as changing the channel to a highlight film of your best wrestling, or the best wrestling performance in the future. For instance, one could imagine they are scoring takedowns, scoring points, and pinning opponents.

Assignment 1.
For the next two weeks, every time something goes wrong in wrestling or life, even the littlest thing like stubbing your toe, use one of the two methods above to stop the negativity. This should give you about 50 reps a day of *negative thought stopping* by flashing the stop sign or changing the channel. After two weeks you will likely be very good at stopping negative thoughts and will begin to see improvements in your performance as you engage in it on the mat. This will also raise your confidence.

Assignment 2.
Take a moment and think about your last practice or match. What
negative thoughts did you have? If you have trouble remembering,
what negative thoughts have you had across your career? Being able
to recognize when you are thinking negatively is an important step in
learning how to manage and control those negative thoughts. Write
down your negative thoughts in the space provided.

My Negative Thoughts List

Building Self-Confidence

One of the simplest and fastest ways to build self confidence in wrestling is to create and read positive affirmations. The simple act of reading a statement like "I AM STRONG" once a day begins to work its way into our subconscious and eventually, we start to believe it. Most Olympians and many professional athletes engage in reading their positive sport affirmations at least once a day and most will before practice and events as well. Wrestlers would be wise to do it as well.

Affirmations are positive 'can do' statements to build self-confidence. They start with the following:

- 'I am'
- 'I have'
- 'I will'
- 'I feel'
- 'I always

For example:
"I always stay in the moment so I can do my best."
"I always have emotional control."
"I am strong."
"I dominate the standup."
"I have great takedown setups."
"I always have great footwork."
"I have the skills to win!"
"I have great pinning skills!"

Write down 10 Positive Affirmations:

1.

2.

3.

4.

5.

6.

7.

8.

9.

10.

Assignment

Type up your list and make 3 copies. Put one on your bathroom mirror, one inside your training bag and the last inside your travel bag. Also put it in a memo on your phone. Read this list when you get up in the morning and right before training or matches to develop more self-confidence.

Accomplishments List

Another simple and fast tool for gaining and regaining self-confidence is the creation of a list of your wrestling and life accomplishments. These should be statements that fill you with pride. When a wrestler is feeling down, they can read this list and be reminded of all the great things they have done in wrestling and life which improves their self-confidence.

For example: "I earned all-conference status" or "or "I won the state tournament" or "I routinely beat people ranked above me." Some wrestlers will even use a very old accomplishment such as "I was the fastest girl/boy in my fourth-grade track day." These can also include life accomplishments like volunteering for charity. As long as the statement reminds you of the pride you felt doing it, it's good.

Write down your 10 greatest accomplishments:

1.

2.

3.

4.

5.

6.

7.

8.

9.

10.

Assignment

Type up your accomplishments in a memo on your phone. If you are feeling down or have low self-confidence read your accomplishments list. You can also read it more often if you like to raise your confidence.

The affirmations and accomplishments lists are based on those presented by Bull, Albinson, and Shambrook (2006).

Break Up the Match

Endeavour to break up the training or match into its smallest components. In training this could be by drill or by attack or by defend. In a match this could be skirmishes/contacts or even move sets. If you win more of these small components and score more points than your opponent, you will typically win the match as long as you don't get caught (and let's face it…everyone gets caught at some point). Consider a move set as both the setup and the actual move, or a setup and the actual takedown attempt. Being able to set up opponents greatly enhances your chances for success on the actual move.

The problem is that most wrestlers look at wrestlers as one big chunk and if they make a mistake, they often can't recover their confidence. This is because thinking this way magnifies mistakes. When mistakes are magnified, they damage our self-confidence more than if they were viewed as smaller components of the match like successful moves. Further, when those mistakes take on greater significance, they tend to create more mistakes, resulting in a domino or snowball effect until the wrestler is soundly defeated. The great thing about wrestling and other combat sports is that no matter how bad a match is going for you as long as you maintain confidence you can always catch an opponent and gain a victory by pin or points. Even if they were badly outscored and out wrestled. Never give up simply because a match is going poorly. If anything, double down and catch your opponent by taking a risk and attacking.

TIPS
If a wrestler makes a mistake, it is essential that the wrestler let go of her/his mistakes, both to save confidence and also to push yourself to keep wrestling. It's best to have a short memory for mistakes. Learn from them and quickly move on to WIN the next move set.

Always stay in the moment and compete one move set or attack at a time. If it fails, simply move to the next move set with confidence.

Assignment

Remind yourself to "Win this move", "Win this takedown", "Win this attack" whenever you feel your focus isn't where it should be and after a mistake. Write some others that you can say to yourself that might work for you.

Performers Focus

Lack of focus is one of the biggest problems that reduce performance in wrestling. Lack of focus can not only result in poor performance, but it can also result in injury. If your mind isn't in "the moment" and is on other things like post-match/tournament parties, work, homework, significant other, your family, or your coach's approval, there is a strong likelihood that you will miss the cues you need to make the move you need to gain victory. You could also miss seeing the cues that allow you to avoid significant injuries that would knock you out of the tournament and possibly result in time away from wrestling.

Ask yourself, what is the most important part of wrestling in regard to focus? Most wrestlers say it is when you are physically exerting yourself offensively or defensively. However, we find that most of the time, when wrestlers are highly trained, this is something that is more automatic…that the moves occur somewhat via instincts and conditioned responses that you learned via years of training and drilling. The most important part is the time from the *end of one move set to the start of the next.* There are important seconds there for positioning, and mental preparation. Similarly, small breaks in wrestling due to a match reset or out of bounds situation are opportunities to gain or maintain focus. It is this repositioning and mental preparation that has the biggest effect on whether an individual will perform well on the upcoming skirmish/contact. A similar concept (McGuire's, 2012; From the Whistle to the Snap) has been used in American football for nearly a decade with great success. It uses these moments to develop your performer's focus and a bit of active recovery to get your wind back.

To create a performer's focus, utilize these small breaks in time to engage in the five steps to focusing below before the action begins again. You don't have to get to all five in a single break but at least do one or two, hopefully more.

Steps to focusing:

1. *Stay in the Moment* – be right here, right now! The past isn't controllable…it no longer matters since we can't change it…so let it go. The future (i.e., the outcome) isn't controllable either so ignore it. Focus on your attitude, communication, and effort (A.C.E.) What are your ABC's (see technique 16)? Ask yourself *"What's Important Now (W.I.N.)"*

2. *Positive Affirmations* – boost your own self-confidence by reminding yourself that you are great, and YOU'VE GOT THIS! See technique 12 for positive affirmation techniques.

3. *Get in Your Zone* – perform your arousal management check and adjust your arousal if necessary. See technique 6 for arousal management techniques. You can also focus on reducing your heart rate to help manage physical fatigue.

4. *Concentrate* – see it, feel it, trust it. See the cues and visualize success. Feel the match in your visualization. Trust that you can do it…that you can replicate your visualization. See technique 3.

5. *Confidence* – confidence is a choice…make the right one. Sometimes saying a cue phrase to yourself like *"I GOT THIS"* or *"TOP QUALITY Wrestling"* can help us make this choice. Another example would be *"ZERO TALENT REQUIRED (Z.T.R.)* since it doesn't take talent to show effort (technique 19).

As you practice this focusing routine it will become something that happens naturally and very quickly (about 1-6 seconds). wrestling should make this a habit.

Assignment
Begin developing your performers focus by using the steps to focus. Make it a habit in practice and then utilize it in matches.

Performers focus is adapted from McGuire (2012).

Routines

Routines help build and improve performance. They give us something to ground ourselves in that we can control. Routines can also allow us to better deal with distractions and adversity. A routine typically includes every <u>significant</u> thing you do, eat, or think about prior to a match. This includes things you do to focus on performing and things done to distract yourself from the stress of competing. If you find yourself having a great match or tournament, think about your routine of that day and repeat it in the future to strengthen your chances of having more great matches.

Assignment: Write down all the things you do to prepare for a match or tournament. Include an approximate time before game such as T-1hour, T-30 min, etc.

Pre- Practice or Game Routine

- Bedtime
- Wake Up
-
-
-
-
-
-
-
-
-
-
-
-
-
- T-10...
- Practice or Match

Having a well-developed routine is highly beneficial to performance. However, we also need to have the ability to adapt (shorten or lengthen) should our normal routine be impossible. For instance, a power outage can wreak havoc on a wrestler's pre-match routine because of the added downtime. Conversely, a late arrival may shorten your preparation time causing difficulties as well. The ability to adapt to such irregularities is a highly desirable skill in all sports.

TIP
I have found that one of the most useful tools in pre-match and tournament routines is the use of games like Mario kart and Smash Bros. Interestingly, both can help us increase arousal because they require us to be focused and attentive. They can also help decrease anxiety and calm us down because they assist us in not thinking about upcoming matches which might stress us out.

Assignment
In the space provided list out the steps to your between-match routine for tournaments. Make sure to include imagery where appropriate.

The ABC's of Mindfulness

Mindfulness is a mental state achieved by focusing your awareness on the present moment. Being *in the moment* means that you are entirely focused on right here, right now; you accept your own feelings, thoughts, and body sensations (including pain) and embrace them. Being mindful during practices and games can significantly improve performance.

<u>The basics of mindfulness practice</u>

1. Set aside some practice time – focus on being completely in the moment. Practice off the mat before you try it on the mat. Practicing off the mat will also make you better on the mat once you use this in competition.

2. Observe the present as it is – pay attention to the moment without judgement.

3. Let judgements go – judgements only cloud our ability to focus and perform well.

4. Return to the present when your mind drifts to other thoughts – if your mind wanders…that's ok…just bring it back to the present (the back and forth is good practice).

A big problem that occurs wrestling is that some wrestlers have a tendency to simply go through the motions of their training. Coach tells you to do something and you simply do it without thinking about it. If we don't think about what we are doing, we don't improve very much. We're simply going through the motions and not being mindful. The adage "practice makes perfect" doesn't actually work....it is more like "thoughtful practice makes perfect." To combat this tendency, I suggest that wrestlers create ABCs for every training session or match.

The ABCs are a simple list of what you need to do today (the present) to have a successful training session, or match. Below is an example of an ABC for a match.

    A. Move your feet, set up the takedown.
    B. Gain Top control.
    C. Set up the pin and hit it hard.

How does a wrestler use this?
For a training session, ask yourself if you completed your ABCs after each drill. If you did not complete them sufficiently then commit more to achieving those ABCs the next drill.

For a match, you should always know your ABC's for every opponent. At high levels these ABCs are effectively your strategy. After a match assess your performance on your ABCs.

In sum, utilizing the ABC's simplifies wrestling and allows the wrestler to be mindful and get the most out of their practices and matches; dramatically increasing their overall development and performance across their career.

Assignment

What are your personal ABCs for training this week? What about your next match or tournament?

Training

     A.

     B.

     C.

Match

     A.

     B.

     C.

Tournament

     A.

     B.

     C.

The ABCs of mindfulness are adopted from Miller (2016).

Post Evaluations

Post evaluations are a highly effective tool for analyzing your performance after training sessions and matches. Many professional athletes, Olympians, and wrestlers use this technique to push through the grind and both maintain confidence and keep training with purpose. Basically, after a training session or match the wrestler lists three things they did well on the top half of a piece of paper. Then on the bottom half they list three things that they could have done better. These things can be physical, mental, technical, or tactical.

Once finished the wrestler reads these items. The good items (strengths) enhance the wrestler's self-confidence as a reminder of what they do well. Many wrestlers will keep these in a folder or notebook to look at when they've had a bad performance or are in a plateau phase of performance. Many athletes complete these post evaluations for every practice and game/match for years. At any time, these athletes can look over the things they consistently do well to raise their self-confidence. It is a powerful pick me up.

The items on the bottom of the page; those that they could have done better, are basically our weaknesses and are read and then made into a focus area for the next training session...they may become ABCs. After committing to that focus, they usually tear the bottom half off the notebook and toss them away to let these weaknesses go so they do not dwell on them.

Assignment
Complete one week's worth of post evaluations. Write them in the space provided and decide on the focus of your next day's practice. Instead of tearing the page simply put a large 'X' over the bottom half once you have committed to focusing on those items in the following days practice. At the end of the week review the things you consistently do well.

Evaluation 1

<u>Things I did well:</u>

-

-

-

<u>Things I could have done better:</u>

-

-

-

Evaluation 2

Things I did well:

-

-

-

Things I could have done better:

-

-

-

Evaluation 3

Things I did well:

-

-

-

Things I could have done better:

-

-

-

Evaluation 4

<u>Things I did well:</u>

-

-

-

<u>Things I could have done better:</u>

-

-

-

Evaluation 5

Things I did well:

-

-

-

Things I could have done better:

-

-

-

Evaluation 6

Things I did well:

-

-

-

Things I could have done better:

-

-

-

Evaluation 7

Things I did well:

-

-

-

Things I could have done better:

-

-

-

Target Goal Setting

Target goal setting is a visual representation of your goals. Goals help us with our motivation and development. We know that the most important goal is your daily goal, shown below at the bullseye of the target. If you meet your daily goal, you'll be more likely to reach your weekly goals, those weekly goals help you meet your monthly goals, and so on with your yearly goals, and dream goals. Too often wrestlers only focus on their dream goal. Dream goals motivate us, but they don't help us get to the dream goal as well as focusing our energy on our daily goals. Daily goals empower us to achieve that dream goal.

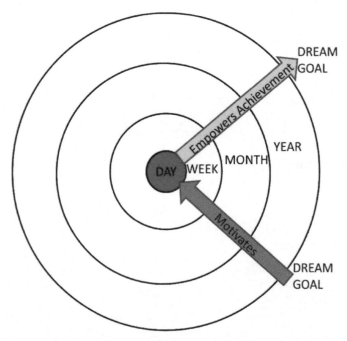

Remember there are many thousands of wrestlers who dream of winning an NCAA championship. That's their goal. However, just dreaming doesn't get the job done. We must meet our daily goals to move toward that dream.

Assignment

Post the target on your wall & list your goals. When finished, post your goals on your wall at home and in your locker. Add them to your phone. Read your goals before practicing each day, paying particular attention to your daily goals. Attempt to make your goals specific, measurable, adjustable, realistic, and set a day in which you feel you can reach that goal.

Daily Goals
-
-
-
-
-
  -

Weekly Goals
-
-
-
-

Monthly Goals
-
-
-

<u>Yearly Goals</u>
-

-

<u>Dream Goal</u>
-

Target goal setting is based on the work of Smith (1999).

Red Head / Blue Head

The concept of Red Head / Blue Head was made famous by Rugby's New Zealand All Blacks (the winningest sport organizations in history…across over 100 years). The idea is that we have two states of mind: Red head and Blue head.

Red Head

Red Head is characterized as HOT (heated, overwhelmed, and tense). These conditions can leave wrestlers tight, inhibited/tentative, anxious, aggressive, and/or desperate. These wrestlers are often result-oriented and over-compensating (i.e., try to do too much). As you can guess, Red Head players typically perform poorly.

Think about your performances. How do you know when you are Red Headed?

-
-
-
-
-
-
-
-
-

Blue Head
Blue Head is characterized by feeling loose, expressive, and *in the moment*. These wrestlers are calm, clear-headed, accurate, and on-task. Blue Head players usually perform well.

What helps you to be Blue Headed on the mat?

-
-
-
-
-
-
-
-

There are several techniques to stay Blue Headed:

1. <u>Mantra's</u> – Mantras are 3 words phrases that may help a wrestler center themselves and direct themselves toward the goal and stay blue headed and perform their best.

   - ZTR – <u>Z</u>ero <u>T</u>alent <u>R</u>equired
   - TQW – <u>T</u>op <u>Q</u>uality <u>W</u>restling
   - FTS – <u>F</u>irst <u>T</u>o <u>S</u>core
   - LQS – <u>L</u>ightening <u>Q</u>uick <u>S</u>hots
   - IGT – <u>I</u> <u>G</u>ot <u>T</u>his

What mantra's do you use?

2. <u>Maps</u> – Maps are a reference for what to do in a situation, (like a pilot experiencing engine failure using a manual to try to restart the malfunctioning engine) they offer clarity in times of stress helping us stay *blue head.*

    Make an "if, then" scenario.
    If _____ then _____.

Assignment

List some "if, then" scenarios that are important for your wrestling in the space below. For example, If *I get taken down* then *I must fight from all positions to escape or get a reversal*.

3. <u>Anchors</u> – Anchors are something that are stable to focus on to keep a *Blue Head*. These anchors are always there for you regardless of the score or your current performance.

- The mat under your feet, feel it with your toes, feel the grip of your shoes on the mat
- The scorer's table beside the mat
- The feel of your singlet.
- Staring into the distance at your countries flag
- The sight of your coach

These anchors act like a reset away from the pressure filled images and thoughts. These are things that support you and give you comfort.

Assignment

What are your anchors that help you stay blue-headed? If you don't have any create some.

A Note on "Legacy" by Kerr. I truly feel that this is one of the best books to teach coaches and players about leadership and the creation of a winning culture. I know scores of coaches in all sports who feel the same way about the book.
Red head / Blue Head, Mantras, Maps, and Anchors are based on the work of Kerr (2013).

Unrealistic Expectations
By Rebecca Case-Lawler, CMPC

Unrealistic expectations can be a very common trait for wrestlers and is a characteristic of perfectionism. Perfectionism can be very dangerous because a wrestler will generally set excessively high standards or expectations of performance that demand either flawless or perfect execution of skills or outcome. This often results in the wrestler becoming overly critical in his/her evaluation of their performance and a heightened sensitivity to making mistakes. In fact, there are two types of "perfectionism" that wrestlers should be aware of:

Positive Perfectionism - a more *flexible* manner of perfectionism... the wrestler strives for excellence and success, sets high goals, however, recognizes his/her own limitations. The key word to remember is *flexible*... wrestlers with positive perfectionism adapt and are flexible with their goals and standards.

Negative Perfectionism – a very *rigid and inflexible* form of perfectionism. Wrestlers routinely set unrealistic and unattainable goals for performance leaving them extremely vulnerable to emotional distress, anger, over-generalizations of perceived failures, and negative self-criticism. The key words to remember are *rigid and inflexible*... wrestlers with negative perfectionism are rarely satisfied with their performance or outcome and measure self-worth solely on successes or failures. These individuals are highly susceptible to self-confidence issues, poor performance and burn-out. And burn-out often leads to quitting the sport.

Seven ways to handle unrealistic expectations / perfectionism:

1. Adopt a "Growth" Mindset- see your mistakes and failures as part of the path to success. As John Wooden, the coach of all coaches used to say, "Mistakes are the steppingstones of success." Without mistakes and losses, we don't improve.

2. <u>Be Aware of Your Thoughts</u> – dwelling on negative thoughts and/or outcomes can quickly spiral out of control becoming monsters of the mind. Catching them quickly and keeping them positive can help combat the monsters.

3. <u>Make a Compare and Contrast List</u>- write down a list of all the negative thoughts, fears, worries, frustrations, judgements, and/or criticisms you may have about a performance, match or tournament. Counter these statements by building a list of positive statements or powerful thoughts. For instance, "I stink at this skill" can be changed to "If I work hard, I will be great at this skill."

4. <u>Set Task-Oriented Goals</u> – task-oriented goals focus on the process of executing skills, not on the outcome. Perfectionists often set outcome- and results-oriented goals, becoming frustrated and angry when they do not achieve perfection. If we focus on the task, the outcome usually takes care of itself. So, remember process over outcome.

5. <u>Build Your "Be Kind to Yourself" Muscle</u> - how we talk to ourselves is just as important as how we talk to our friends, family, and coaches. Most wrestlers, when asked, would never talk to their friends, family, or coaches in a harsh, negative manner. Therefore, talk to yourself in kind and positive ways. This positive self-talk builds our confidence and helps us feel good about our training and performances.

6. <u>W.I.N.</u> - This acronym stands for "What's Important Now," and it means simply staying in the present moment… literally, *the right now* and not becoming fixated on past mistakes or future outcomes. We do not have a time machine to change the past or future so learn from the past and then let it go. The future isn't predetermined so focus on your <u>process</u> – "right here, right now" and the future will take care of itself.

7. <u>Develop your GRIT</u> – setbacks, difficulties and obstacles are inevitable in sport and life. Developing the ability to keep moving forward during times of hardship is a crucial element of GRIT. Often in history, people have put aside their personal interests and used GRIT to accomplish great things or survive during trying times.

Based on the works of: Besharat & Shahidi (2010); Davis, Eshelman, & McKay (2008), Delisio, Lauer, Shigeno, & Lin (2017), Duckworth (2016), and Flett & Hewitt (2005, 2014).

Tips for Managing Pressure

- <u>Breathe</u>. The very act of deep breathing from the diaphragm can relax us both on the mat and off. Ideally our exhale through the mouth should be approximately twice as long as our inhale through the nose. As you exhale allow your stress, anxiety, nervousness, and frustration to leave your body. If you have time, engage in progressive muscle relaxation.

- <u>Control the controllables</u>. Focus your energy only on what you have direct control over. Things like attitude, communication, effort, preparation, nutrition.

- <u>Keep the monkey on your back small.</u> Got a monkey on your back? ... Let it go! Let go of the past and worries about the future. If you don't, that monkey is going to grow to become a 600lb silverback gorilla hanging off your back! Nobody can compete or train with a gorilla on their back.

- <u>Butterflies</u>. Perception is very important in wrestling. We can perceive our pre-match butterflies as threatening and a symptom of pressure or we can perceive them as a signal that we are excited to play. I choose to perceive that they are flying in formation like the blue angels, signaling that I'm excited and ready.

- <u>Keep perspective</u>. Wrestling isn't bigger than life itself. As important as it is, it is still just a sport. Remember, your performance doesn't define you as a person... and you can be a great person longer than you can be a great wrestler.

- <u>Stay in the moment</u>. Be completely engaged in your training and competing. If your mind is on the future or stuck in the past, you will miss the opportunities of the present. Focusing on the past and future only stresses wrestlers out, causing them to perform poorly.

- <u>Fake it until you make it.</u> Even if you aren't confident…fake it. Fake it until your confidence returns. Talk to your sport psychologist and professor about it. The last thing you want to do is give your opponents the fuel for their fire. If they spot your lack of confidence, they will target you.

- <u>Seek out help from your support network</u>. Talking about your problems is cathartic and can help you overcome them. Talk to your sport psychologist or coach. These people want to help you.

- <u>Focus on your own performance.</u> Don't focus on what other people have or what they are doing. Be the best you that *you* can be…because everyone else is already taken. Be Authentic!

- <u>Engage your relaxation skills regularly</u>. Develop and maintain your ability to relax. Relaxation is one of your lifelines in sport. Don't be afraid or too prideful to use it.

- <u>Revisit achievements and success</u>. When you are feeling down look back at your own achievements and successes. Watch highlight film of yourself to remind you how good you actually are.

- <u>Always remember that you are skilled and competent.</u> You wouldn't be at this level if you weren't. You are here for a reason. If you stick with it and work hard good things will come.

A Champions Resilience
By Sarah Charles, MS

There will be many challenging situations that you will come across in wrestling; and performing at an optimal level is key. This will test your mental game tremendously. When we practice our mental game to be on top, we also need to facilitate the ability to recover from mistakes, setbacks, and even failures to accomplish our goals. One area that you need to develop is your resilience. Resilience is the ability to bounce back, grow, flourish, and succeed in the face of a challenge or adversity. Many wrestlers would like to live a life free of failure and adversity. However, just like completing all your reps in the gym to break down and rebuild muscles we also need to experience setbacks and adversity and learn to overcome them in wrestling and life. In being resilient, we want to break down our barriers to uncover how to maintain performance when we experience adversity. Think of resilience like a tennis ball, the tennis ball can absorb shock, it is malleable but does not change form and when you bounce down hard it comes back and bounces even higher. The opposite end is the egg, if you throw down an egg, what happens to it? It breaks, it becomes a pile of goo. We know that being a pile of goo does not bode well for success in wrestling. So how can you be the ball and not the egg? Here are a few things you need to consider.

1) <u>Be flexible</u>: We know that there are going to be many ups and downs in wrestling, so the first step is to be able to manage it and taking the good with the bad in stride. Sometimes we must 'embrace the suck' rather than get 'stuck in the suck.' If you have ever been surfing or watched it, you will notice that one of the most important things is to ride the wave by watching it and making adjustments along the way to stay on the board. That is precisely the same mentality that you need to have when any setback comes along. We need to roll with the constant changes in wrestling. Being static and stuck in a single system or stuck in a certain amount of offensive or defensive pressure will not allow you to wrestle your best or reach your goals.

2) <u>Focus on the Good:</u> It is easy to look at failure and think about all the mistakes and shortcomings that come with that failure. While it is important to look for the things that went wrong, it is imperative not to stay there. Focus on what went well and how you can continue to replicate that and how can the failure be a good thing. What did you learn and what did it provide? Remember that the good things you did don't always appear on the stat line or the podium. Things like hustle, attitude, & effort, for example, are intangibles that make or break a wrestler.

3) <u>Ask a Noble friend:</u> Get perspective by asking others for their insight whether it is a sport psychologist, coach, a mentor, a teammate, or a friend. Resilience thrives on other people. Resilience is absolutely a team sport; it requires the ability to ask for help and use it to push forward in all your endeavors. Take their feedback with an open mind and make the adjustments to improve your wrestling skills.

<u>Assignment</u>: List one area this week where you can be more flexible, focus on the good, and ask a noble friend for feedback.

- Flexibility:

- Good things:

- Noble Friend:

Managing BIG Injuries
By Rebecca Case-Lawler, CMPC

Unfortunately, every wrestler, at some point, will experience an injury. While some injuries are minor, and the wrestler can quickly return to performing, others can be more severe, knocking the wrestler out of wrestling for weeks, months, or even years. The wrestler is then left to not only deal with the physical pain of injury, but also, the emotional loss of wrestling that was so much a part of their identity. In fact, research shows that anger and depression are the most common reported emotions felt when athletes suffer severe injuries. Recovery itself is a difficult process.

Some tools that may help you manage a BIG injury:

- <u>Understand your injury</u> – Knowledge is power! Have your doctor or athletic trainer educate you on the severity and limitations of your injury and the steps you will need to take to safely return to sport. This knowledge can assist in removing many of the anxieties and uncertainties wrestlers might feel during their recovery.

- <u>Have a positive / optimistic attitude</u> – While it may be hard when facing a BIG injury, the attitude you choose concerning your injury will set a standard for your rehabilitation and recovery. For example, speaking confidently to yourself using a mantra such as, "I can", or "I will," helps to fight intrusive thoughts that are disruptive to your progress. Additionally, try to exude confidence to yourself and others by walking with your head up and shoulders back. If you can't walk due to your injury show confidence as you use your crutches. Injury is simply another hurdle along your wrestling path. Attack it with the same confidence you attack training and competition.

- <u>Set goals</u> – Goal setting is a road map of where you are going. Work with your doctor or athletic trainer to set short, medium, and long-term goals right after your injury. This will give you a sense of hope and provide daily motivation to push you through your recovery and adhere to your recovery plan.

- <u>Maintain what you can</u> – You may find that you must cut back on your training considerably when injured or cease it altogether. Finding alternative ways to exercise and maintain your general fitness can be an invaluable tool in maintaining your confidence. For example, a wrestler with a stress fracture in her/his foot may not be able to train; however, he/she could use swimming to maintain a general level of cardiovascular fitness. Another option is an upper body arm cycle to maintain cardiovascular and upper body fitness. Weights are another option.

- <u>Train your brain</u> – You may be limited in your physical abilities however, the time away from wrestling can be a tremendous opportunity to master such skills as, imagery, positive self-talk, relaxation, breathing techniques etc....giving you a mental edge upon return to wrestling. Wrestlers might also endeavor to become students of wrestling by reading wrestling books. Watch technique videos like those from various elite collegiate programs and camps that teach more uncommon styles and moves.

- <u>Have a good team around you</u> – Surround yourself with family, friends, or coaches that are supportive and believe in YOU! Toxic personalities that create doubts and fears about your return to sport drain your energy at a time when you need positive encouragement the most. Avoid those toxic people. It is best to surround yourself with people who give you *"just right support."*

Based on the writings of Taylor, Stone, Mullin, Ellenbeker, & Walgenbach (2003).

Team Travel Tips

The rigors of traveling for tournaments has a wide range of effects on wrestlers, most of which can affect performance. Traveling wrestlers must deal with changes in time zone, altitude, weight cut, hydration levels, recovery, nutrition, and sleep. Basically, the faster one can adapt to their new environment the better they will likely perform. The following guide is to assist you with your travels:

Travel Preparation
Wrestlers should have a checklist of all the items they need for the trip that will be contained in their kit. This assists us in being as comfortable as possible and helps prevent us from forgetting our gear. It's an awful feeling to forget your gear, for example, head gear, and have to borrow someone else's for the tournament.

In addition to clothing and bathroom essentials, I suggest including several other items in your kit.
- Essential travel paperwork (passport, driver's license, etc.).
- Wrestling equipment including a spare pair of essential items
- Recovery items such as foam rollers, and massage guns.
- Weight cut items, suck as sweats or red-light therapy belts.
- Phone and its charger. Most athletes also bring a battery pack.
- Laptop or tablet for reading and entertainment
- Handheld game system (if you typically use one)
- Reading materials (like this book)
- Tape and scissors
- Band-aids or a small first aid kit
- Your pillow
- Any mental tools such as affirmations or ABCs or affirmations that you might need
- Medications (if you have any)

Travel Nutrition

During travel the human body becomes dehydrated. Wrestlers should endeavor to drink a full liter of water during a 2–4-hour flight or drive. This may need to be modified for weigh in. Failing to do so can lead to dehydration, headaches, and fatigue.

Wrestlers should eat during travel. This might have to be after weigh-in. Endeavor to eat foods that are high in carbohydrates for energy for the upcoming event. Starches, grains such as cereal, bread, crackers, rice, potatoes, and pasta are great. So are fresh fruit, and fat-free or low-fat milk and yogurt. During a tournament you will need to refuel between matches as well and should include some protein for recovery. Bananas are helpful sources of carbs since they also prevent cramping. If you are in a multi-day event after your final day one. match immediately consume protein for recovery along with carbs for energy for day two. Make sure to hydrate throughout the tournament.

Avoid caffeine, alcohol, and chocolate because they have diuretic effects and harm our ability to sleep. Avoid all junk food and fast food. Focus on eating salt free nuts, fruits, and vegetables for snacks. Bread heavy sandwiches are acceptable if they are relatively healthy. Low fat high quality, high carb foods are the best. If you must eat fast food, pick something like a good deli sandwich rather than a poor-quality taco. It would be far better to schedule stops at walk-in restaurants with high quality meals.

Traveling

I suggest wrestlers set watches to their destination time zone as soon as they board the plane or bus. If you don't wear a watch, make sure your phone is set to automatically change time zones. Double check that it and any other electronic devices like tablets and laptops are reading correctly upon arrival at your destination. Try to eat and sleep on the schedule of the city you are traveling to and do so for the duration of your stay. The sooner you get your body's schedule to match that of your destination the better off you will be. Some wrestlers begin this process a day or two ahead of time. For the most important tournaments the wise wrestler will start this process up to a week in advance for the best performance.

If you are traveling from west to east sleep very little during travel. Upon arrival sleep 8-10 hours when you go to bed at the appropriate time of your destination. When traveling from east to west sleeping on the plane or drive is encouraged. Think of this sleep as supplemental, like a nap allowing you to stay up until your normal bed at your destination's time zone. However, you do not want to sleep so much that you cannot sleep that night.

Mentally concentrate on controlling the controllables. Travel is unpredictable at best, and often stresses coaches and wrestlers out. Instead of stressing out, roll with the challenges and adapt to the situation. If you have a complete kit, you'll likely have the means to adapt and conquer. Remember that at any time you can engage in imagery to distract yourself from the rigors of travel…imagine yourself making great plays. Always remember to stay positive. Ideally, we want to adapt to our new surroundings as soon as possible. Often scheduling a light practice or walk through upon arrival can enhance performance.

Adapted from Smith (1999).

Professionalism

A quick note on Professionalism. Professionalism can be thought of as the characteristics of a professional. However, these characteristics will be different for each sport. Time and time again I have seen athletes fail to be professional in their pursuit of excellence. Be it troubles with staying eligible to play, troubles with the law, arguments with coaches, motivational challenges, commitment, or even GRIT. It is truly sad to see an athlete squander their talent and the work they have put in but fail to reach their potential for the above-mentioned reasons. My best advice is to look toward highly regarded veteran wrestlers & coaches. Coaches and wrestlers who have the reputation for doing it right and model yourself after them. Don't forget to use common sense as well.

I offer the following tips.
- 100% effort 100% of the time. If you are not 100% healthy, give 100% of whatever you have, always.

- Be accountable – Always be accountable for your actions. Especially the soft moments. For example, if you miss a shot or get caught the fault is your own…not your coach or the referees. You cannot hope to get better and eliminate such mistakes unless you hold yourself accountable.

- Do the Extras. Extras are all the other things you need to do off the mat to be great. Things like watching wrestling, film work on opponents & yourself, preparation, weight training & conditioning, stretching, nutrition, lifestyle (i.e., sleep). These are essential things that many wrestlers don't realize until it's too late.

- Control the controllables.

- Never be too big to sweep the sheds and do the little things to help out. Make yourself indispensable. Indispensable wrestlers often find themselves with opportunities.

- Accept feedback openly and make the adjustments to your wrestling. DO NOT become defensive to the feedback.

- Try to be the first one in and the last one out of training and put that time toward getting better.

- Remember the old adage, nothing good happens after midnight.

- Commitment – You must commit to wrestling and yourself. Whenever an athlete doesn't fully commit to whatever they are doing the chances of failure and injury dramatically increase. Wrestling is a physical sport and it's going to go very badly if we don't go all out and commit to the moves. You are going to be sore, get bruises, and be hurt sometimes anyway...you might as well win the contested moment so commit to it.

- Get better or get beaten. This is the harsh reality of wrestling. If you don't continue to improve there is always someone else coming to take your spot.

- Plant seeds, for it is the seeds you plant today through your hard work, leadership, and mentorship of younger athletes that will bear fruit in the future when your wrestling career is over.

- Have fun. When players lose their sense of fun while practicing and playing, they tend to lose their motivation to perform. wrestling and life are much easier when you are having fun.

The Wrestling Edge

<u>Final Thoughts</u>

As you move forward with the techniques covered in *The Wrestling Edge*, know that if you practice and hone these techniques, they will be there for you when you need them in training, matches, and life. Also know that there are many other mental training techniques available. These can be found working with mental conditioning coaches (CMPC) like myself, or other highly trained individuals. There really is no limit on how much we can train our minds to excel at wrestling. I wish you the best in all of your future wrestling endeavors and always remember to have fun.

Acknowledgements

Thank you to the following people who without their help this book would not have been possible:

- Coach Jeff Buck, Cherokee Trail High School

- Sonny and Cody Yohn, Mile High Wrestling

- Sarah Charles, Mental Performance Consultant, The Performance Mindset

- Rebecca Lawler, CMPC; Author/Editor, Lawler Sport and Performance Consulting

- Dr. Diane Wiese-Bjornstal, Dr. Darren Treasure, and Dr. Aynsley Smith for their mentorship over the past 20+ years

- Photo Credits

  o Kim with Kids In Motion Sports Photography
  https://www.facebook.com/KidsInMotionSportsPhotography/?locale=hi_IN&p aipv=0&eav=AfZIVZ11dlaEf6S7Wal_gU_frAXxzUr1SlQTttqyOt4yNAQWY 5iHxYmqsufCkM4-Sf4&_rdr

  o All parents who donated photos of their wrestlers.

Thanks To all the wrestlers featured in this book!

Featured Wrestlers

- Cover - Ellis Williams
- Pg. 7 - Max Gonzales, Zeke Silva, Derek Glenn, Jr., Josh Richardson, Sam Hart, Matthew Buck, Julian Williams
- Pg. 11 - Coaches Jeff Buck & Seth Bogulski
- Pg. 13 - 2021-22 CT Varsity Wrestling Team
- Pg. 15 - Matthew Buck
- Pg. 19 - Unknown
- Pg. 26 - Ellis Williams
- Pg. 27 - Jay Everhart
- Pg. 29 - Jay Everhart
- Pg. 39 - Matthew Buck
- Pg. 43 - Ellis Williams
- Pg. 46 - Finn O'Riley, Nate Jackson, Kyle Schumann, Derek Glenn, Jr., Zack Fish, Jay Everhart, Matthew Buck
- Pg. 47 - Kyle Stevens, Jay Everhart
- Pg. 51 - Unknown
- Pg. 53 - Jay Everhart, Chance Mathews
- Pg. 55 - Jay Everhart
- Pg. 61 - Unknown
- Pg. 66 - Sam Hart
- Pg. 69 - Jay Everhart
- Pg. 83 - Matthew Buck, Derek Glenn, Jr., Zack Fish
- Pg. 85 - Noah Collins
- Pg. 86 - Unknown
- Pg. 87 - Matthew Buck
- Pg. 91 - Dominique Fish
- Pg. 92 - Matthew Buck
- Pg. 94 - Ellis Williams
- Pg. 97 - Chance Mathews
- Pg. 102 - Unknown
- Pg. 105 - Zaylen Collins, Landon Eckenroth, Chance Mathews, Ellis \ Williams
- Pg. 106 - Jordan Trujillo
- Pg. 107 - Ellis Williams
- Pg. 110 - 2022-23 CT Wrestling Team
- Back Cover – 2021-2022 CT Wrestling Team

About the Author

Jim Winges, Ph.D. CMPC, CC-AASP is a Mental Conditioning Coach and Performance Enhancement Consultant for Titan Sport Performance. Jim works with athletes both nationally and internationally at all levels of sport. Over the past twenty-two years Jim has presented to, taught, and worked with over 5,000 athletes many of whom achieved their goals of state, national championship, professional championships, collegiate scholarships, national team selection and professional and Olympic participation. He has worked with athletes in all major professional sports and was the first Mental Conditioning Coach to work in Major League Rugby. Jim has also conducted trainings for over 5,000 coaches and over 1,800 parents. Jim also works with universities, businesses, the US Military, the US Government, and other organizations to enhance many aspects of performance.

Jim obtained bachelor's degrees from the University of Minnesota-Duluth, a master's degree from Arizona State University and a doctorate from the University of Minnesota-Twin Cities. In addition to his private practice, *Titan Sport Performance*, Jim also taught collegiately for 20 years at a variety of universities. He has also taught a variety of courses for the University of Minnesota-Duluth, Arizona State University, National American University, University of Minnesota, Concordia University, Minnesota State University-Mankato, Louisiana State University & Southeastern Louisiana University.

As an athlete Jim competed in football, ice hockey, wrestling, basketball, & baseball. He is a martial arts practitioner and enjoys snowboarding, surfing, skateboarding, motorsports, biking, fishing and coaching ice hockey. Most of all he enjoys spending quality time with his daughter Ali. His greatest accomplishment is being a father to an amazing daughter.

Jim can be reached at:
612-281-8575
jwinges@gmail.com
www.facebook.com/Titan-Sport-Performance-1531757693598631

Resources

Besharat, M.A. & Shahidi, S. (2010). Perfectionism, anger, and anger rumination. *International Journal of Psychology, 45*(6), 427-434.

Bull, S.J., Albinson, J.G., and Shambrook, C.J. (2006). *The Mental Game Plan: Getting Psyched for Sport.* Sports Dynamics. Cheltenham, UK.

Davis, M., Eshelman, E.R. & Mckay, M. (2008). *The relaxation & stress reduction workbook* (6th ed.). Oakland, CA: New Harbinger Publications, Inc.

Delisio, D., Lauer, E.E., T. Shigeno, & P.Lin. (2017). Building a brotherhood: Neophyte consultants' experiences of working with a high school football program. *Association for Applied Sport Psychology Conference Abstracts.*

Dweck, C.S. (2008). *Mindset: The New Psychology of Success.* Ballantine Books. New York, NY.

Duckworth, A., (2016). *GRIT. The power of passion and perseverance.* New York, NY: Scribner, An Imprint of Simon & Schuster, INC.

Flett, G.L. & Hewitt, P.L. (2005). The perils of perfectionism in sport and exercise. *Current Directions in Psychological Science, 14*(1), 14-18.

Flett, G.L. & Hewitt, P.L. (2014). A proposed framework for preventing perfectionism and promoting resilience and mental health among vulnerable children and adolescents. *Psychology in the Schools, 51* (9), 899-912.

Kerr, J. (2013). *Legacy: What the All Blacks Can Teach Us About the Business of Life.* Constable. London, UK.

Landers, D.M., & Arent, S.M. (2010). Arousal-Performance Relationships. In J.M. Williams (Ed.), *Applied Sport Psychology: Personal Growth to Peak Performance* (6th ed., pp.221-246). Dubuque, IA: McGraw-Hill.

McGuire, R. (2012). *From the Whistle to the Snap: Winning the Mental Game of Football.* Championship Productions. Ames, IA.

Miller, S.L. (2016). *Hockey Tough: A Winning Mental Game.* 2nd ed. Human Kinetics. Champaign IL.

Smith, A.M. (1999). *Power Play: Mental Toughness for Hockey and Beyond.* 3rd ed. Athletic Guide Publishing. Rochester, MN.

Taylor, J., Stone, K.R., Mullin, M.J., Ellenbecker, T., Walgenbach, A. (2003). *Comprehensive sports management: From examination of injury to return to sport.* (2nd ed.). Austin, TX: Pro-Ed.

Weinberg, R.S., & Gould, D. (2015). *Foundations of Sport and Exercise Psychology. 6th ed.* Human Kinetics. Champaign, IL.

Williams, J.M., & Krane, V. (2015). *Applied Sport Psychology: Personal Growth to Peak Performance* 6th ed. McGraw-Hill. Dubuque, IA.

Clipart Image
www.mycutegraphics.com/graphics/monster/three-eyed-monster.html

Notes

Notes

Notes

Notes

Notes

Made in the USA
Monee, IL
11 October 2024

67616880R00066